The Birds
of
Harlowedge Lane

Barboursville, Virginia

photographer and author
Bobbie Montana

Love and thanks to my husband
for all his support for my hobby.

All Glory to God

-tufted titmouse

-male Eastern bluebird

-dark-eyed junco

Many and varied

-black capped chickadee

-male yellow-bellied sapsucker

-male and female housefinches

the birds on Harlowedge Lane

-male American goldfinch

come to my feeders

-male housefinch
and
male American goldfinch

outside my window pane.

-male and female cardinals

Bright red cardinals

-male and female cardinals

pose just so,

-male cardinal and Eastern song sparrow

and dance on wings before they go.

Rusts and browns

*-male cardinal
and
indigo bunting*

and indigo blue

*—male cardinal
and
female ruby-throated
hummingbirds*

and tiny darting hummingbirds, too.

-male and female
ruby-throated
hummingbirds

Velvet greens, a glimpse of red

*-female
ruby-throated
hummingbirds*

graceful choreography

before being fed.

-bluejay

Suddenly swoop, dark blues and white

like a speeding bullet to get a bite.

-bluejay and female cardinal

There's no room here for him to sit,
so he flew away with a small tidbit.

-juvenile
Cooper's hawk

Majestic hawk shows off for me

*-juvenile Cooper's hawk
and squirrel*

then chases a squirrel up a tree.

-Carolina wren

Baby wrens are quickly fed.

-brown thrasher

-female downy woodpecker

-male hairy woodpecker

More browns and blacks and a spot of red.

-male red-bellied woodpecker

A bright red cap caught my eye.

*-female and male
red-bellied
woodpecker*

Grab some seeds and off they fly.

-male red-breasted grosbeak

Sweetly singing in the branches

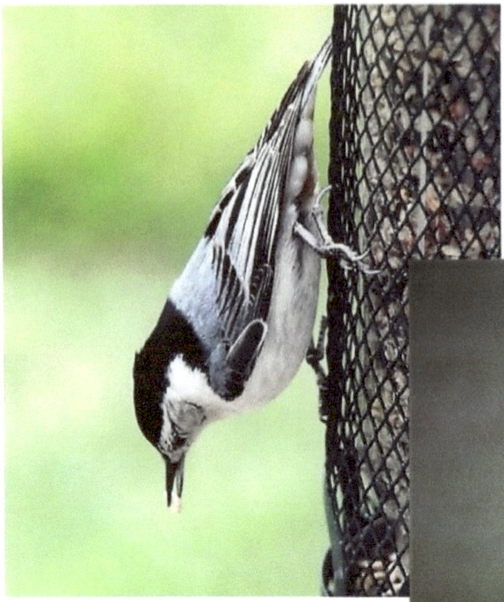

-white breasted nuthatch

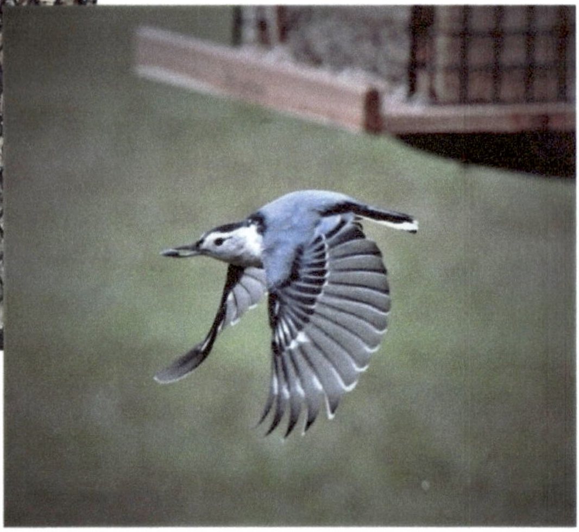

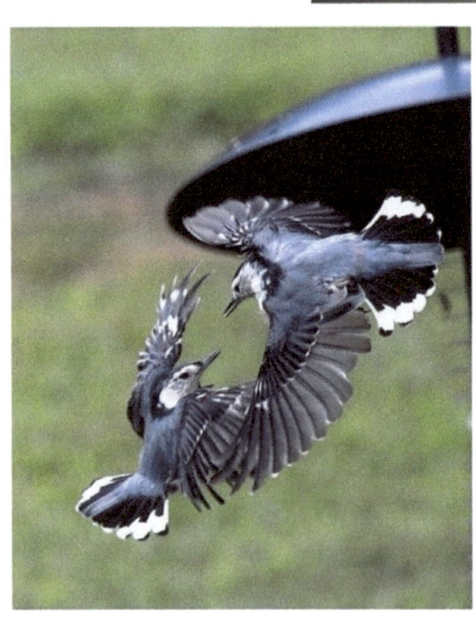

while the nuthatch madly dances.

-*Eastern bluebird*

The bluebird fiercely guards his home,

-male Eastern bluebird

before he wings on high

-juvenile and male Eastern bluebird

to feed the fledgling getting ready to roam.

-*male pileated woodpecker*

An old stump is the landing pad
for this handsome woodpecker lad.